Summer is Here!

Helena Ramsay

Illustrated by
Annabel Spenceley

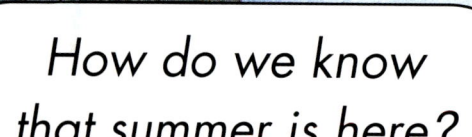

Swallows come here when it's warm and there are plenty of insects for them to eat.

Birds' eggs hatch in the spring. By summer the babies are ready to fly.

"The strawberries are nice and ripe."

In summer the hot sun
ripens the strawberries.

Wasps have black and yellow stripes to warn other animals that they are dangerous.

15

Roses flower in the summer.
They have a lovely scent.

Butterflies like the scent of the flowers, too.

Soon it will ripen in the sun. Then it will be ready for the farmer to harvest.

We need to water the garden in summer because there isn't very much rain.

The sun is still shining!

In summer the days are long and the nights are short. Bed time stays the same though!

   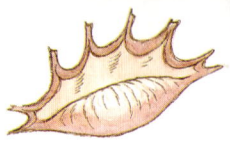

"Tomorrow we're going to have some more summer fun."

These are the things we see in the summer.
Can you name them?